This copy of

A PRAYER FOR THE OPENING
OF THE LITTLE LEAGUE SEASON

is presented to

_____

by

_____

_____

Date

PRAYER FOR T[

Willie Morris

PENING OF THE LITTLE LEAGUE SEASON

Illustrated by Barry Moser

HARCOURT BRACE & COMPANY
SAN DIEGO · NEW YORK · LONDON

Library of Congress Cataloging-in-Publication Data
Morris, Willie.
A prayer for the opening of the Little League season/Willie
Morris; illustrated by Barry Moser.—1st ed.
p. cm.
ISBN 0-15-200892-6
ISBN 0-15-200781-4 (ltd. edition)
1. Little league baseball—Juvenile poetry. 2. Baseball
for children—Juvenile poetry. I. Title.
PS3563.O8745P73   1995
811'.54—dc20   94-14471

First edition   A B C D E

Printed in Singapore

OR OUR FRIEND, JOHN EVANS:
who is either a literary man who loves baseball, or a
baseball man who loves literature, or both.

—W.M. & B.M.

DEAR ALMIGHTY GOD,

HIS IS A prayer for all the kids of all races and creeds in the boundless earthly springtime as baseball once more commences, as it has and will eternally in the ordinance and charter of Thy inexorable seasons.

FIRST, bless the youthful catchers—in their awkward knee pads and chest pads and masks, their unwieldy tools of ignorance, which shelter all the boys who possess the valor to be catchers—that they may be safe from injury and neglect, from errant curveballs and stray fast ones and sharp little fouls that nip the mortal flesh.

PROTECT the little infielders from bad bounces and assuage the pain of wounded lips and cheeks when blood mingles with the infield soil; grant them deft shovel dips and 6-4-3 double plays.

SPARE THE eager outfielders from misjudging long drives in the lengthening twilight, permit them swift, diving catches in the dry and tranquil grass, and assure them hard, accurate tosses on cutoff throws to the inmost diamonds, straight to second, or at the corners with the runners going.

SAVE THE young pitchers from all erratic affliction as the line drives whip past their heads and torsos and toes, and give them mastery of their fastballs and curves, that they may outwit the fledgling enemy sluggers, especially with men on the bases.

IMPART faith to the rookies whose toil is to wait in the bullpens, where their labor is anonymous, as it has been through mortal time, that they, too, shall inherit the earth, for theirs is a lonely calling.

COMFORT the smallest of the ball-players, who have never gotten a hit, and those who strike out time and time again or languish on the benches day after livelong day, for their moment, too, is destined to be.

DEFEND the little ballplayers, when they drop flies or boot grounders, from the wrath of their fathers, for many are the fathers who fear not the timeless injunction "Judge not, that ye be not judged." Forever shield the erring boys from retributive daddies who know not even the Infield Fly Rule.

EWARD the faithful mothers as they transport their children to practice, launder their sullied uniforms, soothe their cuts and bruises, pacify their anxious qualms, and sustain them in triumph as in adversity with cheers and acclamations from the bleachers, for theirs is rightfully the Kingdom of Heaven.

GLORIFY, too, the grandparents in their faithfulness and the aunts and uncles who bear witness in the stands, and forsake not the little brothers and sisters who admire their agile siblings with an abiding eagerness.

ABSOLVE the umpires from the consequences of their flaws, bequeath them transcendent vision, and sanctify them above all for the close calls at the plate, for they, more than any of Thy creatures, are afflicted with tribulations.

REMIND US that baseball will never die, for its everlasting rhythms lie rooted in the soil and its passions, in the smell of the new grass, in the hot sunshine of the deepest summers, in the enduring chatter that ripples through the bleachers, in the wafting odor of peanuts and popcorn and breaded corn dogs.

ABOVE ALL, grant us boyhood and girlhood, where in time's soft reverie we are forever children, and where baseball shall dwell with us always, and where sharp grounders are eternally fielded in a new leather glove and drives to deep center are ceaselessly ensnared in shoestring catches and the wicked curveballs are met with two-run singles to left-center, to win the game in the bottom half of the ninth.

IN THY INFINITE wisdom and grace, our Great Umpire in the Heavens, grant all this in perpetuity to all the baseball children of the earth.

AMEN